THIS COCKTAIL RECIPE BOOK BELONGS TO:

MY AWESOME COCKTAIL RECIPES

RECIPE	PAGE

MY AWESOME COCKTAIL RECIPES

RECIPE

PAGE

MY AWESOME COCKTAIL RECIPES

RECIPE ──────────────────────────────────

PAGE

MY AWESOME COCKTAIL RECIPES

RECIPE

PAGE

MEASUREMENT CONVERSION CHART

CUPS, SPOONS & LIQUIDS

MEASURE	OUNCES	EQUIVALENTS	LITERS
1/4 tsp			1 ml
1/2 tsp			2.5 ml
1 tsp		1/3 Tbsp	5 ml
2 tsp	1/3 fl oz	2/3 Tbsp	10 ml
1 Tbsp	1/2 fl oz	3 tsp	15 ml
2 Tbsp	1 fl oz	1/8 cup (6 tsp)	30 ml
1/4 cup	2 fl oz	4 Tbsp	60 ml
1/3 cup	2 2/3 fl oz	5 Tbsp & 1 tsp	80 ml
1/2 cup	4 fl oz	8 Tbsp	120 ml
2/3 cup	5 1/3 fl oz	10 Tbsp & 2 tsp	160 ml
3/4 cup	6 fl oz	12 Tbsp	180 ml
7/8 cup	7 fl oz	14 Tbsp	200 ml
1 cup (1/2 pint)	8 fl oz	16 Tbsp	220 ml
2 cups (1 pint)	16 fl oz	32 Tbsp	250 ml
1 quart	32 fl oz	4 cups	950 ml
1 quart plus 1/4 cup	34 fl oz	4 cups & 4 Tbsp	1 L
1 gallon (4 quarts)	128 fl oz	16 cups	3.8 L

WEIGHT

OUNCES	POUNDS	GRAMS
1/4 ounce		7 g
1/2 ounce		15 g
3/4 ounce		21 g
1 ounce		28 g
2 ounces		57 g
3 ounces		85 g
4 ounces	1/4 pound	113 g
8 ounces	1/2 pound	227 g
16 ounces	1 pound	454 g
35.2 ounces	2.2 pounds	1 kg

TEMPERATURE

FAHRENHEIT	CELSIUS
250° F	120° C
275° F	140° C
300° F	150° C
325° F	160° C
350° F	180° C
375° F	190° C
400° F	200° C
425° F	220° C
450° F	230° C
475° F	245° C

COCKTAIL ....

📅 DATE .... DIFFICULTY ⭘⭘⭘⭘⭘ RATING ☆☆☆☆☆

INGREDIENTS

_____

_____

_____

_____

_____

_____

_____

_____

_____

_____

DIRECTIONS

_____

_____

_____

_____

_____

_____

_____

_____

_____

_____

_____

_____

🍷 GLASS

🌿 GARNISH _____

_____

_____

📝 NOTES _____

_____

_____

_____

_____

7

COCKTAIL ....

📅 DATE ....   DIFFICULTY ○ ○ ○ ○ ○   RATING ☆ ☆ ☆ ☆ ☆

🍾 INGREDIENTS

....
....
....
....
....
....
....
....
....
....
....

🍸 DIRECTIONS

....
....
....
....
....
....
....
....
....
....
....
....
....
....
....

🍷 GLASS

🌿 GARNISH ....
....
....
....

📝 NOTES ....
....
....
....
....

8

COCKTAIL ....

INGREDIENTS

_____
_____
_____
_____
_____
_____
_____
_____
_____
_____
_____
_____

DIRECTIONS

_____
_____
_____
_____
_____
_____
_____
_____
_____
_____
_____
_____

GLASS

GARNISH _____
_____
_____

NOTES _____
_____
_____
_____

COCKTAIL ....

📅 **DATE** .... **DIFFICULTY** ○○○○○ **RATING** ☆☆☆☆☆

🍾 **INGREDIENTS**

🍸 **DIRECTIONS**

🥂 **GLASS**

🌿 **GARNISH** ....

📝 **NOTES** ....

COCKTAIL ....

📅 **DATE** .... **DIFFICULTY** ○○○○○ **RATING** ☆☆☆☆☆

INGREDIENTS

....
....
....
....
....
....
....
....
....
....
....

DIRECTIONS

....
....
....
....
....
....
....
....
....
....
....
....

GLASS

GARNISH ....
....
....

NOTES ....
....
....

COCKTAIL

01 DATE .... DIFFICULTY ○○○○○ RATING ☆☆☆☆☆

INGREDIENTS

DIRECTIONS

GLASS

GARNISH

NOTES

COCKTAIL ....

INGREDIENTS

DIRECTIONS

🍷 GLASS

💐 GARNISH ....
....
....

📔 NOTES ....
....
....
....

COCKTAIL ....

📅 DATE .... DIFFICULTY ○ ○ ○ ○ ○ RATING ☆ ☆ ☆ ☆ ☆

INGREDIENTS

....
....
....
....
....
....
....
....
....
....

DIRECTIONS

....
....
....
....
....
....
....
....
....
....
....
....

GLASS

GARNISH ....
....
....
....

NOTES ....
....
....
....
....

14

COCKTAIL ....

INGREDIENTS

DIRECTIONS

GLASS

GARNISH ....

NOTES ....

COCKTAIL ....

📅 **01** DATE ....   DIFFICULTY ○ ○ ○ ○ ○   RATING ☆ ☆ ☆ ☆ ☆

🍾 **INGREDIENTS**

....	....
....	....
....	....
....	....
....	....
....	....
....	....
....	....
....	....
....	....
....	....

🍸 **DIRECTIONS**

....
....
....
....
....
....
....
....
....
....
....
....
....

🍷 **GLASS**

🌿 **GARNISH** ....
....
....

📝 **NOTES** ....
....
....
....

16

COCKTAIL

📅 DATE _____   DIFFICULTY ○○○○○   RATING ☆☆☆☆☆

INGREDIENTS

DIRECTIONS

GLASS

GARNISH

NOTES

COCKTAIL

01 DATE .... DIFFICULTY ○ ○ ○ ○ ○ RATING ☆ ☆ ☆ ☆ ☆

INGREDIENTS

DIRECTIONS

GLASS

GARNISH

NOTES

COCKTAIL

DATE .... **DIFFICULTY** ○○○○○ **RATING** ☆☆☆☆☆

INGREDIENTS

DIRECTIONS

GLASS

GARNISH

NOTES

COCKTAIL

DATE .... DIFFICULTY ○ ○ ○ ○ ○ RATING ☆ ☆ ☆ ☆ ☆

INGREDIENTS

DIRECTIONS

GLASS

GARNISH

NOTES

COCKTAIL

01 DATE .... **DIFFICULTY** ○ ○ ○ ○ ○   **RATING** ☆ ☆ ☆ ☆ ☆

INGREDIENTS

DIRECTIONS

GLASS

GARNISH

NOTES

COCKTAIL ....

01 DATE ....   DIFFICULTY ○ ○ ○ ○ ○   RATING ☆ ☆ ☆ ☆ ☆

INGREDIENTS

DIRECTIONS

GLASS

GARNISH ....

NOTES ....

COCKTAIL ....

📅 **DATE** .... DIFFICULTY ○○○○○ RATING ☆☆☆☆☆

🍾 **INGREDIENTS**

🍸 **DIRECTIONS**

🍷 **GLASS**

🌿 **GARNISH** ....

📝 **NOTES** ....

COCKTAIL

DATE .... DIFFICULTY ○○○○○ RATING ☆☆☆☆☆

INGREDIENTS

DIRECTIONS

GLASS

GARNISH

NOTES

COCKTAIL ....

DATE .... DIFFICULTY ○○○○○ RATING ☆☆☆☆☆

INGREDIENTS

DIRECTIONS

GLASS

GARNISH ....
....
....

NOTES ....
....
....
....

25

COCKTAIL

DATE .... DIFFICULTY ○ ○ ○ ○ ○   RATING ☆ ☆ ☆ ☆ ☆

INGREDIENTS

DIRECTIONS

GLASS

GARNISH

NOTES

COCKTAIL ....

📅 **01** DATE .... DIFFICULTY ○○○○○ RATING ☆☆☆☆☆

🍾 **INGREDIENTS**

....
....
....
....
....
....
....
....
....
....
....

🍸 **DIRECTIONS**

....
....
....
....
....
....
....
....
....
....
....
....
....
....

🍷 **GLASS**

🌿 **GARNISH** ....
....
....

📓 **NOTES** ....
....
....
....

COCKTAIL

01 DATE _____   DIFFICULTY ○ ○ ○ ○ ○   RATING ☆ ☆ ☆ ☆ ☆

INGREDIENTS

DIRECTIONS

GLASS

GARNISH

NOTES

COCKTAIL ....

01 DATE .... DIFFICULTY ○○○○○ RATING ☆☆☆☆☆

INGREDIENTS

_____
_____
_____
_____
_____
_____
_____
_____
_____
_____
_____

DIRECTIONS

_____
_____
_____
_____
_____
_____
_____
_____
_____
_____
_____
_____

GLASS

GARNISH ....
....
....
....

NOTES ....
....
....
....

COCKTAIL

01 DATE .... DIFFICULTY ○ ○ ○ ○ ○ RATING ☆ ☆ ☆ ☆ ☆

INGREDIENTS

DIRECTIONS

GLASS

GARNISH

NOTES

COCKTAIL ....

DATE .... **DIFFICULTY** ○ ○ ○ ○ ○ **RATING** ☆ ☆ ☆ ☆ ☆

INGREDIENTS

DIRECTIONS

GLASS

GARNISH ....
....
....
....

NOTES ....
....
....
....
....

COCKTAIL ....

📅 DATE .... DIFFICULTY ○ ○ ○ ○ ○ RATING ☆ ☆ ☆ ☆ ☆

🍾 INGREDIENTS

🍸 DIRECTIONS

🍷 GLASS

🌿 GARNISH ....
....
....

📝 NOTES ....
....
....
....

32

COCKTAIL ....

📅 DATE .... DIFFICULTY ⭕⭕⭕⭕⭕ RATING ☆☆☆☆☆

🍾 INGREDIENTS

🍸 DIRECTIONS

🍷 GLASS

🌿 GARNISH ....

📝 NOTES ....

COCKTAIL

DATE .... DIFFICULTY ○ ○ ○ ○ ○   RATING ☆ ☆ ☆ ☆ ☆

INGREDIENTS

DIRECTIONS

GLASS

GARNISH

NOTES

34

COCKTAIL ....

DATE .... **DIFFICULTY** ○ ○ ○ ○ ○   **RATING** ☆ ☆ ☆ ☆ ☆

INGREDIENTS

DIRECTIONS

GLASS

GARNISH

NOTES

COCKTAIL

01 DATE _____   DIFFICULTY ○○○○○   RATING ☆☆☆☆☆

INGREDIENTS

_____
_____
_____
_____
_____
_____
_____
_____
_____
_____
_____
_____

DIRECTIONS

_____
_____
_____
_____
_____
_____
_____
_____
_____
_____
_____
_____
_____
_____

GLASS

GARNISH _____
_____
_____
_____

NOTES _____
_____
_____
_____
_____

COCKTAIL ....

🗓 DATE .... DIFFICULTY ○ ○ ○ ○ ○ RATING ☆ ☆ ☆ ☆ ☆

INGREDIENTS

DIRECTIONS

GLASS

GARNISH ....
....
....

NOTES ....
....
....
....

COCKTAIL ....

📅 DATE ....   DIFFICULTY ○ ○ ○ ○ ○   RATING ☆ ☆ ☆ ☆ ☆

INGREDIENTS

....
....
....
....
....
....
....
....
....
....
....
....

DIRECTIONS

....
....
....
....
....
....
....
....
....
....
....
....
....
....

GLASS

GARNISH ....
....
....

NOTES ....
....
....
....

COCKTAIL

01 DATE ....   DIFFICULTY ○○○○○   RATING ☆☆☆☆☆

INGREDIENTS

DIRECTIONS

GLASS

GARNISH

NOTES

COCKTAIL

....

📅 01 DATE .... **DIFFICULTY** ⭕⭕⭕⭕⭕ **RATING** ☆☆☆☆☆

INGREDIENTS

....	....
....	....
....	....
....	....
....	....
....	....
....	....
....	....
....	....
....	....
....	....

DIRECTIONS

....
....
....
....
....
....
....
....
....
....
....
....
....

GLASS

GARNISH ....
....
....

NOTES ....
....
....
....

COCKTAIL

DATE .... DIFFICULTY ○○○○○ RATING ☆☆☆☆☆

INGREDIENTS

DIRECTIONS

GLASS

GARNISH

NOTES

41

COCKTAIL

DATE

DIFFICULTY ○ ○ ○ ○ ○

RATING ☆ ☆ ☆ ☆ ☆

INGREDIENTS

DIRECTIONS

GLASS

GARNISH

NOTES

42

COCKTAIL ....

📅 DATE .... DIFFICULTY ○ ○ ○ ○ ○ RATING ☆ ☆ ☆ ☆ ☆

INGREDIENTS

DIRECTIONS

🍷 GLASS

🌿 GARNISH ....
....
....
....

📋 NOTES ....
....
....
....

COCKTAIL

📅 DATE .... DIFFICULTY ○ ○ ○ ○ ○ RATING ☆ ☆ ☆ ☆ ☆

INGREDIENTS

....
....
....
....
....
....
....
....
....
....
....

DIRECTIONS

....
....
....
....
....
....
....
....
....
....
....
....

GLASS

GARNISH ....
....
....

NOTES ....
....
....
....

COCKTAIL

DATE .... **DIFFICULTY** ○○○○○ **RATING** ☆☆☆☆☆

INGREDIENTS

DIRECTIONS

GLASS

GARNISH

NOTES

45

COCKTAIL

01 DATE .... DIFFICULTY ○○○○○ RATING ☆☆☆☆☆

INGREDIENTS

DIRECTIONS

GLASS

GARNISH

NOTES

COCKTAIL ....

DATE .... **DIFFICULTY** ○ ○ ○ ○ ○ **RATING** ☆ ☆ ☆ ☆ ☆

INGREDIENTS

DIRECTIONS

GLASS

GARNISH ....
....
....

NOTES ....
....
....
....

47

COCKTAIL

01 DATE ....   DIFFICULTY ○○○○○   RATING ☆☆☆☆☆

INGREDIENTS

DIRECTIONS

GLASS

GARNISH

NOTES

COCKTAIL

DATE .... DIFFICULTY ○ ○ ○ ○ ○   RATING ☆ ☆ ☆ ☆ ☆

INGREDIENTS

DIRECTIONS

GLASS

GARNISH

NOTES

COCKTAIL

DATE .... **DIFFICULTY** ○ ○ ○ ○ ○ **RATING** ☆ ☆ ☆ ☆ ☆

INGREDIENTS

DIRECTIONS

GLASS

GARNISH

NOTES

COCKTAIL ....

DATE .... **DIFFICULTY** ○○○○○ **RATING** ☆☆☆☆☆

INGREDIENTS

DIRECTIONS

GLASS

GARNISH ....

NOTES ....

COCKTAIL

DATE ....   **DIFFICULTY** ○ ○ ○ ○ ○   **RATING** ☆ ☆ ☆ ☆ ☆

INGREDIENTS

....
....
....
....
....
....
....
....
....
....
....
....

DIRECTIONS

....
....
....
....
....
....
....
....
....
....
....
....
....
....

GLASS

GARNISH ....
....
....
....

NOTES ....
....
....
....
....

COCKTAIL ....

INGREDIENTS

DIRECTIONS

GLASS

GARNISH ....
....
....

NOTES ....
....
....
....

COCKTAIL

01 DATE _____   DIFFICULTY ○ ○ ○ ○ ○   RATING ☆ ☆ ☆ ☆ ☆

INGREDIENTS

DIRECTIONS

GLASS

GARNISH

NOTES

COCKTAIL

DATE ....

DIFFICULTY ○ ○ ○ ○ ○

RATING ☆ ☆ ☆ ☆ ☆

INGREDIENTS

DIRECTIONS

GLASS

GARNISH

NOTES

55

COCKTAIL

01 DATE .... DIFFICULTY ○ ○ ○ ○ ○ RATING ☆ ☆ ☆ ☆ ☆

INGREDIENTS

DIRECTIONS

GLASS

GARNISH

NOTES

COCKTAIL

DATE _____   DIFFICULTY ○○○○○   RATING ☆☆☆☆☆

INGREDIENTS

DIRECTIONS

GLASS

GARNISH

NOTES

COCKTAIL

DATE .... DIFFICULTY ○ ○ ○ ○ ○ RATING ☆ ☆ ☆ ☆ ☆

INGREDIENTS

DIRECTIONS

GLASS

GARNISH

NOTES

COCKTAIL

DATE .... DIFFICULTY ○ ○ ○ ○ ○   RATING ☆ ☆ ☆ ☆ ☆

INGREDIENTS

DIRECTIONS

GLASS

GARNISH

NOTES

COCKTAIL

DATE .... DIFFICULTY ○ ○ ○ ○ ○   RATING ☆ ☆ ☆ ☆ ☆

INGREDIENTS

DIRECTIONS

GLASS

GARNISH ....

NOTES ....

COCKTAIL

📅 DATE ....   DIFFICULTY ⭕⭕⭕⭕⭕   RATING ☆☆☆☆☆

INGREDIENTS

.... | ....
.... | ....
.... | ....
.... | ....
.... | ....
.... | ....
.... | ....
.... | ....
.... | ....
.... | ....
.... | ....

DIRECTIONS

GLASS

GARNISH

NOTES

COCKTAIL

01 DATE .... DIFFICULTY ○ ○ ○ ○ ○ RATING ☆ ☆ ☆ ☆ ☆

INGREDIENTS

DIRECTIONS

GLASS

GARNISH

NOTES

COCKTAIL

DATE .... DIFFICULTY ○ ○ ○ ○ ○ RATING ☆ ☆ ☆ ☆ ☆

INGREDIENTS

DIRECTIONS

GLASS

GARNISH

NOTES

COCKTAIL

DATE .... **DIFFICULTY** ○ ○ ○ ○ ○ **RATING** ☆ ☆ ☆ ☆ ☆

INGREDIENTS

DIRECTIONS

GLASS

GARNISH

NOTES

64

COCKTAIL

DATE .... DIFFICULTY ○○○○○ RATING ☆☆☆☆☆

INGREDIENTS

DIRECTIONS

GLASS

GARNISH

NOTES

COCKTAIL

📅 DATE _____   DIFFICULTY ○○○○○   RATING ☆☆☆☆☆

🍾 INGREDIENTS

🍸 DIRECTIONS

🥂 GLASS

🌿 GARNISH _____

📝 NOTES _____

COCKTAIL

DATE .... DIFFICULTY ○ ○ ○ ○ ○   RATING ☆ ☆ ☆ ☆ ☆

INGREDIENTS

DIRECTIONS

GLASS

GARNISH

NOTES

COCKTAIL ....

📅 DATE ....   DIFFICULTY ○ ○ ○ ○ ○   RATING ☆ ☆ ☆ ☆ ☆

🍾 INGREDIENTS

🍸 DIRECTIONS

🍷 GLASS

💐 GARNISH ....
....
....

📝 NOTES ....
....
....
....

COCKTAIL

01 DATE .... **DIFFICULTY** ○○○○○ **RATING** ☆☆☆☆☆

INGREDIENTS

DIRECTIONS

GLASS

GARNISH

NOTES

COCKTAIL ....

📅 **DATE** .... **DIFFICULTY** ○ ○ ○ ○ ○ **RATING** ☆ ☆ ☆ ☆ ☆

🍾 **INGREDIENTS**

🍸 **DIRECTIONS**

🍷 **GLASS**

💐 **GARNISH** ....
....
....

📝 **NOTES** ....
....
....
....

COCKTAIL

DATE .... DIFFICULTY ○○○○○ RATING ☆☆☆☆☆

INGREDIENTS

DIRECTIONS

GLASS

GARNISH

NOTES

71

COCKTAIL

01 DATE .... DIFFICULTY ○ ○ ○ ○ ○ RATING ☆ ☆ ☆ ☆ ☆

INGREDIENTS

DIRECTIONS

GLASS

GARNISH

NOTES

COCKTAIL

DATE _____ **DIFFICULTY** ○ ○ ○ ○ ○ **RATING** ☆ ☆ ☆ ☆ ☆

INGREDIENTS

DIRECTIONS

GLASS

GARNISH

NOTES

COCKTAIL ....

INGREDIENTS

DIRECTIONS

🍷 GLASS

🌿 GARNISH ....

📓 NOTES ....

COCKTAIL

....

📅 DATE ....   DIFFICULTY ⃝⃝⃝⃝⃝   RATING ☆☆☆☆☆

INGREDIENTS

DIRECTIONS

🍷 GLASS

🌿 GARNISH ....
....
....

📝 NOTES ....
....
....
....

COCKTAIL

INGREDIENTS

DIRECTIONS

GLASS

GARNISH

NOTES

COCKTAIL

📅 DATE .... DIFFICULTY ○○○○○ RATING ☆☆☆☆☆

🍾 INGREDIENTS

🍸 DIRECTIONS

🍷 GLASS

🌿 GARNISH

📝 NOTES

COCKTAIL

DATE .... DIFFICULTY ○○○○○ RATING ☆☆☆☆☆

INGREDIENTS

DIRECTIONS

GLASS

GARNISH

NOTES

COCKTAIL

DATE _____ **DIFFICULTY** ○ ○ ○ ○ ○ **RATING** ☆ ☆ ☆ ☆ ☆

INGREDIENTS

_____
_____
_____
_____
_____
_____
_____
_____
_____
_____

DIRECTIONS

_____
_____
_____
_____
_____
_____
_____
_____
_____
_____
_____
_____
_____

GLASS

GARNISH _____
_____
_____

NOTES _____
_____
_____
_____
_____

COCKTAIL ....

📅 **DATE** .... **DIFFICULTY** ○ ○ ○ ○ ○   **RATING** ☆ ☆ ☆ ☆ ☆

🍾 **INGREDIENTS**

🍸 **DIRECTIONS**

🍷 **GLASS**

🌿 **GARNISH** ....

📝 **NOTES** ....

COCKTAIL

01 DATE .... DIFFICULTY ○○○○○ RATING ☆☆☆☆☆

INGREDIENTS

DIRECTIONS

GLASS

GARNISH

NOTES

COCKTAIL

DATE .... DIFFICULTY ○ ○ ○ ○ ○   RATING ☆ ☆ ☆ ☆ ☆

INGREDIENTS

DIRECTIONS

GLASS

GARNISH

NOTES

COCKTAIL

DATE .... **DIFFICULTY** ○ ○ ○ ○ ○ **RATING** ☆ ☆ ☆ ☆ ☆

INGREDIENTS

....
....
....
....
....
....
....
....
....
....
....
....

DIRECTIONS

....
....
....
....
....
....
....
....
....
....
....
....
....

GLASS

GARNISH ....
....
....
....

NOTES ....
....
....
....

COCKTAIL

DATE .... DIFFICULTY ○ ○ ○ ○ ○ RATING ☆ ☆ ☆ ☆ ☆

INGREDIENTS

DIRECTIONS

GLASS

GARNISH

NOTES

COCKTAIL

🗓 DATE .... DIFFICULTY ○○○○○ RATING ☆☆☆☆☆

INGREDIENTS

DIRECTIONS

GLASS

GARNISH

NOTES

COCKTAIL

DATE .... DIFFICULTY ○ ○ ○ ○ ○ RATING ☆ ☆ ☆ ☆ ☆

INGREDIENTS

DIRECTIONS

GLASS

GARNISH

NOTES

COCKTAIL

DATE .... DIFFICULTY ○ ○ ○ ○ ○ RATING ☆ ☆ ☆ ☆ ☆

INGREDIENTS

DIRECTIONS

GLASS

GARNISH

NOTES

COCKTAIL

01 DATE _____   DIFFICULTY ○ ○ ○ ○ ○   RATING ☆ ☆ ☆ ☆ ☆

INGREDIENTS

DIRECTIONS

GLASS

GARNISH

NOTES

88

COCKTAIL

....

📅 DATE .... DIFFICULTY ○○○○○ RATING ☆☆☆☆☆

🍾 INGREDIENTS

....
....
....
....
....
....
....
....
....
....
....

🍸 DIRECTIONS

....
....
....
....
....
....
....
....
....
....
....
....
....

🍷 GLASS

🌿 GARNISH ....
....
....
....

📓 NOTES ....
....
....
....
....

COCKTAIL

01 DATE

DIFFICULTY ○ ○ ○ ○ ○

RATING ☆ ☆ ☆ ☆ ☆

INGREDIENTS

DIRECTIONS

GLASS

GARNISH

NOTES

COCKTAIL

DATE .... DIFFICULTY ○ ○ ○ ○ ○ RATING ☆ ☆ ☆ ☆ ☆

INGREDIENTS

DIRECTIONS

GLASS

GARNISH

NOTES

COCKTAIL

📅 DATE ....   DIFFICULTY ○ ○ ○ ○ ○   RATING ☆ ☆ ☆ ☆ ☆

INGREDIENTS

....
....
....
....
....
....
....
....
....
....
....

DIRECTIONS

....
....
....
....
....
....
....
....
....
....
....
....
....

🍷 GLASS

🌿 GARNISH ....
....
....

📝 NOTES ....
....
....
....

COCKTAIL

DATE

DIFFICULTY ○ ○ ○ ○ ○

RATING ☆ ☆ ☆ ☆ ☆

INGREDIENTS

DIRECTIONS

GLASS

GARNISH

NOTES

COCKTAIL ....

📅 DATE ....   DIFFICULTY ○○○○○   RATING ☆☆☆☆☆

🍾 INGREDIENTS

....
....
....
....
....
....
....
....
....
....
....
....
....

🍸 DIRECTIONS

....
....
....
....
....
....
....
....
....
....
....
....
....
....

🍷 GLASS

🍹 GARNISH ....
....
....

📝 NOTES ....
....
....
....

COCTAIL ....

📅 **DATE** .... **DIFFICULTY** ○ ○ ○ ○ ○ **RATING** ☆ ☆ ☆ ☆ ☆

INGREDIENTS

DIRECTIONS

....
....
....
....
....
....
....
....
....
....
....
....
....

GLASS

GARNISH ....
....
....

NOTES ....
....
....
....
....

COCKTAIL

📅 **DATE** .... **DIFFICULTY** ○ ○ ○ ○ ○   **RATING** ☆ ☆ ☆ ☆ ☆

INGREDIENTS

DIRECTIONS

🍷 **GLASS**

💐 **GARNISH**

📝 **NOTES**

COCKTAIL

DATE _____   **DIFFICULTY** ○○○○○   **RATING** ☆☆☆☆☆

INGREDIENTS

DIRECTIONS

GLASS

GARNISH

NOTES

COCKTAIL

01 DATE .... DIFFICULTY ○○○○○ RATING ☆☆☆☆☆

INGREDIENTS

DIRECTIONS

GLASS

GARNISH ....
....
....
....

NOTES ....
....
....
....

COCKTAIL

DATE .... **DIFFICULTY** ○○○○○ **RATING** ☆☆☆☆☆

INGREDIENTS

DIRECTIONS

GLASS

GARNISH

NOTES

COCKTAIL

DATE

DIFFICULTY ○ ○ ○ ○ ○

RATING ☆ ☆ ☆ ☆ ☆

INGREDIENTS

DIRECTIONS

GLASS

GARNISH

NOTES

100

COCKTAIL

DATE .... DIFFICULTY ○○○○○ RATING ☆☆☆☆☆

INGREDIENTS

DIRECTIONS

GLASS

GARNISH

NOTES

COCKTAIL

📅 **01 DATE** .... **DIFFICULTY** ○○○○○   **RATING** ☆☆☆☆☆

🍾 **INGREDIENTS**

🍸 **DIRECTIONS**

🥂 **GLASS**

🌿 **GARNISH** ....

📝 **NOTES** ....

COCTAIL

....

📅 **DATE** .... **DIFFICULTY** ○ ○ ○ ○ ○   **RATING** ☆ ☆ ☆ ☆ ☆

🍾 INGREDIENTS

🍸 DIRECTIONS

🍷 **GLASS**

🌿 **GARNISH** ....

....

....

....

📝 **NOTES** ....

....

....

....

....

COCKTAIL

INGREDIENTS

DIRECTIONS

GLASS

GARNISH

NOTES

COCKTAIL

01 DATE .... **DIFFICULTY** ○○○○○ **RATING** ☆☆☆☆☆

INGREDIENTS

DIRECTIONS

GLASS

GARNISH

NOTES

COCKTAIL

01 DATE _____   DIFFICULTY ○○○○○   RATING ☆☆☆☆☆

INGREDIENTS

DIRECTIONS

GLASS

GARNISH

NOTES

COCKTAIL

01 DATE .... DIFFICULTY ○○○○○ RATING ☆☆☆☆☆

INGREDIENTS

DIRECTIONS

GLASS

GARNISH

NOTES

COCKTAIL

📅 DATE .... DIFFICULTY ○○○○○ RATING ☆☆☆☆☆

🍾 INGREDIENTS

....
....
....
....
....
....
....
....
....
....
....

🍸 DIRECTIONS

....
....
....
....
....
....
....
....
....
....
....
....
....

🍷 GLASS

🍹 GARNISH ....
....
....

📝 NOTES ....
....
....
....
....

COCKTAIL _____

INGREDIENTS

_____
_____
_____
_____
_____
_____
_____
_____
_____
_____

DIRECTIONS

_____
_____
_____
_____
_____
_____
_____
_____
_____
_____
_____
_____

GLASS

GARNISH
_____
_____
_____

NOTES _____
_____
_____
_____
_____

COCKTAIL ....

📅 **01** DATE .... DIFFICULTY ○ ○ ○ ○ ○ RATING ☆ ☆ ☆ ☆ ☆

🍾 **INGREDIENTS**

_____ _____
_____ _____
_____ _____
_____ _____
_____ _____
_____ _____
_____ _____
_____ _____
_____ _____
_____ _____
_____ _____
_____ _____

🍸 **DIRECTIONS**

_____
_____
_____
_____
_____
_____
_____
_____
_____
_____
_____
_____
_____

🍷 **GLASS**

🌿 **GARNISH** ....
_____
_____

📓 **NOTES** ....
_____
_____
_____
_____

COCKTAIL

DATE .... DIFFICULTY ○ ○ ○ ○ ○ RATING ☆ ☆ ☆ ☆ ☆

INGREDIENTS

DIRECTIONS

GLASS

GARNISH

NOTES

COCKTAIL

01 DATE ....

DIFFICULTY ○ ○ ○ ○ ○

RATING ☆ ☆ ☆ ☆ ☆

INGREDIENTS

DIRECTIONS

GLASS

GARNISH

NOTES

COCKTAIL

📅 DATE .... DIFFICULTY ○ ○ ○ ○ ○ RATING ☆ ☆ ☆ ☆ ☆

INGREDIENTS

DIRECTIONS

🍷 GLASS

💐 GARNISH

📝 NOTES

COCKTAIL

01 DATE .... DIFFICULTY ○○○○○ RATING ☆☆☆☆☆

INGREDIENTS

DIRECTIONS

GLASS

GARNISH

NOTES

COCKTAIL

DATE .... DIFFICULTY ○○○○○ RATING ☆☆☆☆☆

INGREDIENTS

DIRECTIONS

GLASS

GARNISH

NOTES

COCKTAIL

INGREDIENTS

DIRECTIONS

🍷 GLASS

💐 GARNISH

📝 NOTES

COCKTAIL

📅 DATE _____   DIFFICULTY ⭕⭕⭕⭕⭕   RATING ☆☆☆☆☆

INGREDIENTS

DIRECTIONS

🍷 GLASS

🌿 GARNISH _____

📝 NOTES _____

COCKTAIL

01 DATE ....   DIFFICULTY ○○○○○   RATING ☆☆☆☆☆

INGREDIENTS

DIRECTIONS

GLASS

GARNISH

NOTES

COCKTAIL

📅 DATE _____   DIFFICULTY ○ ○ ○ ○ ○   RATING ☆ ☆ ☆ ☆ ☆

🍾 INGREDIENTS

🍸 DIRECTIONS

🍷 GLASS

🌿 GARNISH

📝 NOTES

Contact:

Gerald Curk Marketing & Design
Waldschmidtstraße 9 • 93051 Regensburg
GERMANY

Any questions or suggestions: servus@curk.de

Made in the USA
Monee, IL
19 May 2022

96719946R00073